Building Wealth:

Proven Investment Tactics for Financial Freedom

BY

John M. Woods

About The Author

John M. Woods, a financial virtuoso hailing from the bustling streets of New York City, stands as a beacon of wisdom in the realm of business and finance. With a mysterious air that accompanies his every move, Woods has etched his name into the annals of financial literature, captivating readers with his enigmatic charm and unparalleled insights.

TABLE OF CONTENT

Introduction

Building wealth and achieving financial freedom is a goal that many people aspire to, yet it can often seem elusive and out of reach. In today's ever-changing economic landscape, it is essential to equip oneself with the knowledge and strategies necessary to navigate the world of investments and wealth accumulation effectively. "Building Wealth: Proven Investment Tactics for Financial Freedom" is a comprehensive guide that aims to demystify the process of wealth building and provide proven tactics for securing long-term financial stability.

This book is designed to empower individuals with the tools and understanding needed to make sound financial decisions, regardless of their current financial status. By delving into the psychology of wealth accumulation, debunking common myths, and laying a solid foundation for financial management, readers will gain a holistic understanding of the principles that underpin successful wealth building. From investment strategies for long-term growth to exploring the opportunities presented by real estate, entrepreneurship, and retirement planning, this book offers insights into various avenues for wealth creation.

Furthermore, "Building Wealth" goes beyond conventional investment advice to encompass advanced tactics, such as tax planning, alternative investments, and cultivating a wealth mindset. By adopting a comprehensive approach to wealth building, readers will be equipped to navigate the complexities of the financial world and make informed decisions that align with their long-term goals.

Ultimately, the goal of this book is not just to provide a one-size-fits-all solution, but to empower individuals to craft personalized wealth-building plans that are sustainable and aligned with their unique aspirations. By embracing the wisdom shared within these pages, readers will embark on a journey towards financial freedom and abundance, armed with the knowledge and confidence needed to secure their financial future.

CHAPTER 1

Understanding the Foundations of Wealth

Understanding the foundations of wealth involves gaining insight into the principles and practices that contribute to the accumulation and preservation of financial resources. It encompasses a multifaceted understanding of the psychological, behavioral, and strategic aspects of wealth building.

The Psychology of Wealth Accumulation

The psychology of wealth accumulation explores the mindset, beliefs, attitudes, emotions, and behaviors that influence an individual's relationship with money and their ability to build and maintain wealth. This field of study recognizes that financial decisions are not solely rational, but are often influenced by psychological factors, biases, and emotional responses.

One aspect of the psychology of wealth accumulation involves understanding an individual's mindset towards money. This can be characterized as an abundance mindset, where individuals believe in the availability of opportunities and resources, or a scarcity mindset, where individuals perceive limitations and are driven by fear of lacking. These mindsets can significantly impact financial decision-making and wealth-building behaviors.

Emotions also play a critical role in the psychology of wealth accumulation. Emotional responses such as fear, greed, anxiety, and overconfidence can influence investment decisions, risk tolerance, and financial planning strategies. Understanding and managing these emotions is essential for making rational, informed choices in wealth accumulation.

Additionally, cognitive biases and heuristics, which are shortcuts or mental "rules of thumb" that individuals use to make decisions, have a significant impact on financial behavior. Common biases such as loss aversion, confirmation bias, and anchoring can lead to suboptimal investment decisions and impede long-term wealth accumulation.

Furthermore, the psychology of wealth accumulation considers the impact of upbringing, societal conditioning, and personal experiences on one's relationship with money. Childhood experiences, familial attitudes towards wealth, and cultural influences can shape financial beliefs and behaviors, impacting an individual's approach to wealth accumulation.

In addressing the psychology of wealth accumulation, it is important to develop self-awareness, emotional intelligence, and the ability to recognize and mitigate biases. Building a positive and empowered mindset towards money, understanding emotional triggers, and making rational financial decisions are key aspects of leveraging the psychology of wealth accumulation to support long-term financial success. Additionally, seeking guidance from financial professionals who understand the psychological dimensions of wealth accumulation can provide valuable support in navigating the complexities of financial decision-making.

Defining financial freedom and its significance

Financial freedom can be defined as the ability to make significant life decisions without being unduly stressed about the financial impact of those choices. It is a state of being where an individual has enough wealth and income to live the life they desire, without being overwhelmed by financial constraints.

Significance of Financial Freedom:

1. Reduced Stress: Financial freedom provides peace of mind and reduces stress related to money matters, allowing individuals to focus on other aspects of their lives, such as personal well-being, relationships, and pursuing their passions.

2. Increased Options: With financial freedom, individuals have more options available to them, such as the ability to pursue further education, travel, start a business, or retire early, without being constrained by financial limitations.

3. Independence: Financial freedom fosters a sense of independence, enabling individuals to rely on their own resources rather than being dependent on others or feeling trapped in unfulfilling jobs or situations due to financial necessity.

4. Security: Achieving financial freedom provides a sense of security for both the present and the future. Having savings, investments, and a reliable source of income can help mitigate unexpected financial challenges and provide a safety net for the long term.

5. Fulfillment: Financial freedom allows individuals to align their finances with their

values and goals, leading to a more fulfilling and purposeful life. It provides the freedom to spend time on meaningful activities and experiences that contribute to overall happiness and well-being.

Financial freedom not only impacts an individual's financial well-being but also has positive effects on their mental, emotional, and physical health. It offers the flexibility and freedom to make choices based on personal aspirations rather than financial constraints, ultimately leading to a more satisfying and balanced life.

Identifying and Debunking Common Myths about Wealth Building

Myth 1: You need a high income to build wealth.

Debunked: While a high income can certainly accelerate the wealth-building process, it is not the sole determinant of financial success. Many individuals with moderate incomes have built substantial wealth through disciplined saving, smart investing, and living within their means.

Myth 2: Wealth building requires taking on high levels of risk.

Debunked: While all investments carry some degree of risk, successful wealth building involves a balanced approach to risk management. It's important to diversify investments, avoid putting all eggs in one basket, and understand the risk-return tradeoff. Additionally, wealth can be built steadily through consistent saving and conservative investment strategies.

Myth 3: Inheriting money is the easiest path to wealth.

Debunked: While inheriting wealth can provide a financial boost, it does not guarantee long-term financial security. Effective wealth building involves financial discipline, smart decision-making, and a long-term perspective. Many self-made millionaires and billionaires did not inherit substantial wealth, but rather built it through hard work, perseverance, and sound financial practices.

Myth 4: You need to be an expert in finance to build wealth.

Debunked: While financial literacy is beneficial, you don't need to be a financial expert to build wealth. Basic understanding of saving, budgeting, and investing principles, along with seeking guidance from trusted financial professionals, can help individuals make informed decisions and progress towards their financial goals.

Myth 5: Wealth building is only for the privileged or lucky.

Debunked: Building wealth is attainable for individuals from all walks of life. It requires a combination of discipline, determination, and consistent effort. While external factors may influence opportunities, the habits and mindset around money management play a significant role in building sustainable wealth.

Debunking these common myths about wealth building is crucial in promoting a realistic and inclusive approach to financial success. Understanding that wealth building is achievable through prudent financial habits, informed decision-making, and perseverance can empower individuals to take control of their financial futures.

CHAPTER 2

Setting the Stage: Building a Solid Financial Foundation

Building a solid financial foundation is essential for long-term financial success and stability. It involves establishing fundamental practices and principles that form the groundwork for achieving one's financial goals. This process encompasses various aspects such as budgeting, saving, debt management, investing, and financial literacy.

1. Budgeting: The first step in building a solid financial foundation is creating a realistic and comprehensive budget. A budget helps individuals track their income and expenses, enabling them to prioritize spending, identify areas for saving, and avoid unnecessary debt. It also provides a clear

overview of financial inflows and outflows, facilitating informed decision-making.

2. Saving: Saving money is a key component of financial security. It provides a safety net for unexpected expenses, helps achieve short-term and long-term goals, and lays the groundwork for investment opportunities. Building an emergency fund and setting aside a portion of income for future needs are crucial elements of a solid financial foundation.

3. Debt Management: Managing and reducing debt is essential for financial stability. High-interest debt can hinder wealth-building efforts, so it's important to develop strategies for paying down debts systematically. Prioritizing high-interest debt, consolidating loans, and negotiating with creditors are effective approaches to managing debt effectively.

4. Investing: Once a solid financial base is established through budgeting, saving, and debt management, individuals can consider investment opportunities to grow their wealth. This may involve exploring retirement accounts, diversified portfolios, real estate, or other investment vehicles aligned with their risk tolerance and financial goals.

5. Financial Literacy: Developing a strong understanding of financial concepts and products is vital for making informed decisions. Financial literacy empowers individuals to navigate the complex landscape of personal finance, including taxes, insurance, retirement planning, and investment options. Continuous learning and staying informed about financial matters are integral to building and maintaining a solid financial foundation.

6. Risk Management: Protecting one's financial well-being through insurance and risk mitigation strategies is a critical aspect of a solid financial foundation. This includes having adequate health insurance, life insurance, disability insurance, and other forms of protection to safeguard against unexpected events that could derail financial progress.

Setting the stage for building a solid financial foundation involves a holistic approach to managing finances, encompassing budgeting, saving, debt management, investing, financial literacy, and risk management. By establishing these foundational principles and practices, individuals can lay the groundwork for long-term financial stability, growth, and achieving their financial aspirations.

Budgeting and managing personal finances

Budgeting and managing personal finances are critical components of achieving financial stability and security. Let's delve deeper into these topics to understand their significance and strategies for effective implementation.

Budgeting:

Definition and Purpose:

Budgeting involves creating a plan for how to allocate financial resources, taking into account income, expenses, and savings goals. The primary purpose of budgeting is to provide a clear understanding of where money is being spent and to ensure that spending aligns with financial priorities.

Steps in Budgeting:

- Assessing Income and Expenses: Start by evaluating all sources of income and identifying regular expenses such as housing, utilities, transportation, groceries, and discretionary spending.

- Setting Financial Goals: Determine short-term and long-term financial objectives, such as building an emergency fund, paying off debt, saving for a home or retirement, and allocate funds accordingly.

- Tracking Spending: Record and categorize all expenses to gain insight into spending patterns and identify areas for potential cost-cutting.

- Creating the Budget: Based on income, expenses, and financial goals, establish a budget that allocates specific amounts for each category, ensuring that total expenses do not exceed income.

- Regular Review and Adjustment: Continuously monitor actual spending against the budget, making adjustments as necessary to stay on track and accommodate changes in financial circumstances.

Managing Personal Finances:

Debt Management:

Effective personal finance management involves developing a strategy for managing and reducing debt. This may include prioritizing high-interest debts, consolidating loans, negotiating with creditors, and making timely payments to minimize interest expenses.

Savings and Emergency Fund:

Prioritizing savings is essential for achieving financial security. Building an emergency fund to cover unforeseen expenses, setting aside funds for short-term goals, and contributing to long-term savings vehicles such as retirement accounts are key aspects of managing personal finances.

Investing:

As part of a comprehensive financial strategy, individuals can consider investing to grow their wealth. This may involve exploring various investment options, such as stocks, bonds, mutual funds, real estate, or retirement accounts, aligned with one's risk tolerance and financial goals.

Financial Literacy:

Developing a strong understanding of financial concepts and products is crucial for informed decision-making. Continuous learning about budgeting, saving, investing, taxes, insurance, and other financial topics empowers individuals to make sound financial choices.

Risk Management:

Protecting one's financial well-being through insurance and risk mitigation strategies is essential. This includes having adequate health insurance, life insurance, disability insurance, and other forms of protection to safeguard against unexpected events.

Budgeting and managing personal finances are foundational pillars of financial well-being. By establishing a budget, prioritizing savings, managing debt, exploring investment opportunities, enhancing financial literacy, and implementing risk management strategies, individuals can lay the groundwork for long-term financial stability and achievement of their financial goals.

The importance of debt management

The importance of debt management cannot be overstated when it comes to achieving and maintaining financial stability. Debt, when left unmanaged, can significantly restrict an individual's financial freedom, impact creditworthiness, and hinder long-term financial goals. Let's explore the critical aspects of debt management and its importance in personal finance.

Understanding Debt Management:

1. Debt Awareness: Acknowledging the types and amounts of debt one owes is the first step in effective debt management. This includes various forms such as credit card balances, personal loans, student loans, mortgages, and other financial obligations.

2. Creating a Repayment Plan: Developing a structured plan to pay off debts efficiently involves prioritizing high-interest loans, setting specific payment amounts, and adhering to a payment schedule. This can help reduce the overall interest paid and accelerate the debt repayment process.

3. Budget Integration: Integrating debt repayment into a comprehensive budget

allows individuals to allocate a portion of their income toward servicing debts while still addressing essential living expenses and savings goals.

4. Avoiding Accumulation of New Debt: Concurrently managing existing debt and avoiding the accumulation of new, unnecessary debt is crucial to prevent a cycle of increasing financial burden.

The Importance of Debt Management:

1. Financial Health: Effective debt management is pivotal to maintaining overall financial health. Excessive debt can strain an individual's financial resources and impact their ability to meet their financial obligations and future goals.

2. Creditworthiness: Responsibly managing debt is vital for building and maintaining a

favorable credit score. A good credit history enhances the ability to secure favorable terms for future loans, mortgages, and credit cards.

3. Stress Reduction: Managing debt can alleviate the stress and anxiety associated with financial burdens. By implementing a clear plan to address debt, individuals can regain a sense of control and peace of mind.

4. Pursuing Financial Goals: Uncontrolled debt can impede progress toward achieving important financial milestones such as saving for a home, funding education, or planning for retirement. By effectively managing debt, individuals can redirect funds toward these long-term aspirations.

5. Long-Term Stability: Proactive debt management contributes to long-term financial stability and resilience. It enables individuals to lessen their financial vulnerabilities and build a stronger

foundation for their future financial well-being.

The importance of debt management lies in its ability to safeguard financial health, enhance creditworthiness, reduce stress, support the pursuit of financial goals, and secure long-term stability. By implementing prudent debt management practices, individuals can pave the way for a more secure and prosperous financial future.

Building an emergency fund and creating a safety net

Building an emergency fund and creating a safety net are crucial components of personal financial planning. These measures provide a financial cushion to address unexpected expenses and unforeseen circumstances, offering stability and peace of mind in times of need. Let's delve into the significance and strategies for building an emergency fund and creating a safety net.

Building an Emergency Fund:

1. Purpose: An emergency fund serves as a dedicated pool of funds specifically earmarked to cover unforeseen expenses, such as medical emergencies, car repairs, or unexpected job loss.

2. Fund Size: Financial experts recommend accumulating three to six months' worth of living expenses in an emergency fund. This provides a buffer to handle prolonged periods of income disruption or significant expenses.

3. Consistent Contributions: Regularly setting aside a portion of income, whether monthly or per paycheck, is essential to steadily grow the emergency fund.

4. Liquid and Accessible Assets: The emergency fund should consist of liquid and

easily accessible assets, such as a savings account or money market fund, to ensure swift access when needed.

5. Financial Security: Having an adequate emergency fund instills a sense of financial security, reducing the need to rely on high-interest debt or deplete long-term savings to cover unexpected costs.

Creating a Safety Net:

1. Insurance Coverage: Adequate insurance coverage, including health, property, auto, and life insurance, forms a critical part of a comprehensive safety net. Insurance policies protect against major financial setbacks resulting from accidents, illnesses, or property damage.

2. Debt Management: Effectively managing and reducing personal debt forms another layer of financial protection. Lower debt

levels afford greater financial flexibility during challenging times.

3. Diversified Investments: Diversifying investments across asset classes and maintaining a well-structured investment portfolio can shield against market volatility and economic downturns.

4. Multiple Income Streams: Establishing and nurturing multiple income streams, such as part-time work, freelance projects, or rental income, offers added resilience in the face of job loss or reduced primary income.

Significance of Building an Emergency Fund and Creating a Safety Net:

1. Financial Stability: An emergency fund and a robust safety net provide a stable financial foundation, empowering individuals

to weather unexpected financial shocks without jeopardizing their long-term financial well-being.

2. Reduced Stress: Knowing that there are resources in place to handle unforeseen expenses alleviates stress and anxiety surrounding financial uncertainties.

3. Preventive Measures: By proactively building an emergency fund and creating a comprehensive safety net, individuals can mitigate potential financial crises and minimize the need to resort to high-cost borrowing or liquidation of long-term assets.

4. Long-Term Planning: These measures align with prudent long-term financial planning by safeguarding financial assets and promoting overall financial resilience.

Building an emergency fund and creating a safety net are essential steps in cultivating financial security and resilience. These measures offer protection against unforeseen financial challenges, reduce stress, and enable individuals to navigate through uncertain times with greater confidence and stability.

CHAPTER 3

Investment Strategies for Long-Term Wealth

Investment strategies for long-term wealth refer to the approaches and methods individuals or entities use to grow their wealth over an extended period. The goal is to build a substantial financial portfolio that can provide for future needs, such as retirement or legacy planning. Some common investment strategies for long-term wealth include:

1. Diversification: Spreading investments across different asset classes, such as stocks, bonds, real estate, and commodities, to reduce risk and enhance potential returns.

2. Dollar-cost averaging: Investing a fixed amount of money at regular intervals,

regardless of market conditions. This strategy can help smooth out the impact of market volatility over time.

3. Buy and hold: Purchasing quality assets with the intention of holding onto them for an extended period, often with the belief that their value will increase over time.

4. Rebalancing: Periodically adjusting the investment portfolio to maintain the desired asset allocation, which helps manage risk and ensure that investments align with long-term goals.

5. Retirement accounts: Utilizing tax-advantaged accounts, such as 401(k)s, IRAs, and pension plans, to save and invest for retirement, taking advantage of compounding returns and potential tax benefits.

6. Real estate investment: Investing in income-generating properties or real estate

investment trusts (REITs) to build long-term wealth through rental income and property appreciation.

7. Long-term stock investment: Selecting fundamentally strong companies and holding their stocks for an extended period, benefiting from potential capital appreciation and dividends.

It's important to note that these strategies should be tailored to individual risk tolerance, financial goals, and time horizon. Additionally, seeking advice from financial professionals before implementing any investment strategy is advisable.

Introduction to various investment vehicles (stocks, bonds, real estate)

Investing is a crucial aspect of personal finance and wealth management, offering the potential to grow capital and achieve financial goals over time. The world of investment vehicles encompasses a diverse array of options, each with its unique characteristics, risk-return profiles, and investment strategies. Understanding these investment vehicles is fundamental for individuals seeking to build a well-rounded investment portfolio.

Let's delve into an in-depth exploration of various investment vehicles, including stocks, bonds, real estate, and other options:

1. Stocks:

Stocks represent ownership in a company and are traded on stock exchanges. When you buy stocks, you become a shareholder in the company, which means you have a claim on its assets and earnings. The value of stocks can fluctuate based on factors such as company performance, market conditions, and economic outlook. Investing in stocks can provide potential for high returns over the long term but also involves higher risk due to market volatility.

2. Bonds:

Bonds are debt securities issued by governments, municipalities, or corporations to raise capital. When you purchase a bond, you are essentially lending money to the issuer in exchange for periodic interest payments and the eventual return of the principal amount at maturity. Bonds offer steady income through interest payments and are generally considered less risky than stocks, making them a popular choice for conservative investors seeking stability and regular income.

3. Real Estate:

Real estate investment involves purchasing properties with the expectation of generating income through rental payments or property appreciation over time. Real estate can provide diversification to an investment portfolio and serve as a hedge against inflation. Additionally, real estate investment trusts (REITs) offer an opportunity to invest in real estate assets without owning physical properties, providing liquidity and diversification.

4. Mutual Funds:

Mutual funds pool money from multiple investors to invest in a diversified portfolio of stocks, bonds, or other securities. They are managed by professional fund managers who make investment decisions on behalf of the investors. Mutual funds provide diversification, professional management, and liquidity, making them attractive for investors seeking a convenient way to access a variety of investment opportunities.

5. Exchange-Traded Funds (ETFs):

ETFs are similar to mutual funds but trade on stock exchanges like individual stocks. They offer diversification, low costs, and intraday trading flexibility. ETFs can track specific indexes, sectors, or asset classes, providing exposure to a wide range of investment options in a single investment vehicle.

6. Commodities:

Investments in commodities, such as gold, silver, oil, and agricultural products, provide a way to diversify a portfolio and hedge against inflation. Commodities can be invested in directly or through commodity-based mutual funds, ETFs, or futures contracts, offering exposure to the performance of global commodity markets.

7. Options and Futures:

Options and futures are derivative securities that derive their value from an underlying asset, such as stocks, bonds, or commodities. They offer opportunities for hedging, speculation, and leveraging investment positions, but they also involve complex strategies and carry higher risk due to their leveraged nature.

These investment vehicles vary in terms of risk, return potential, liquidity, and complexity, so it's important for investors to carefully consider their financial goals, risk tolerance, and investment time horizon when selecting the most suitable options for their portfolios. Additionally, seeking professional financial advice is recommended to ensure that investment choices align with individual circumstances and objectives.

Diversification and risk management

Diversification and risk management are fundamental concepts in the world of investing, playing a crucial role in constructing a well-balanced investment portfolio and minimizing the impact of market volatility. By diversifying investments across various asset classes, sectors, and geographical regions, investors can manage risk and potentially improve their overall risk-adjusted returns. In this comprehensive exploration, we will delve deeply into the concepts of diversification and risk management, examining their significance, strategies, and practical applications in the realm of investment.

Diversification:

Diversification is the strategy of spreading investments across different asset classes, industries, and securities to reduce exposure to any single investment. The goal of diversification is to lower the overall risk of a portfolio by mitigating the impact of adverse events that may affect specific assets or sectors. This approach is based on the principle that not all investments will perform in the same way at the same time, and therefore, spreading capital across a range of assets can help balance out the overall portfolio performance.

Significance of Diversification:

1. Risk Reduction: Diversification aims to minimize the impact of individual investment risk on the overall portfolio. By holding a mix of assets with low or negative correlations, the portfolio becomes less susceptible to extreme fluctuations in value.

2. Enhanced Consistency: Diversification can lead to more consistent returns over time, as losses in one asset or sector may be offset by gains in another. This can lead to a smoother, less volatile investment experience.

3. Opportunity for Growth: By investing in different asset classes and sectors, investors

can position themselves to capitalize on opportunities for growth in diverse areas of the market. This can help optimize the overall risk-return profile of the portfolio.

Strategies for Diversification:

1. Asset Allocation: Allocating investments across different asset classes such as stocks, bonds, real estate, and commodities is a fundamental aspect of diversification. Each asset class has its unique risk-return profile, and combining them can help mitigate overall portfolio risk.

2. Sector Allocation: Within equity holdings, diversifying across various industry sectors (e.g., technology, healthcare, consumer goods) can help reduce the impact of sector-specific risks.

3. Geographic Diversification: Investing in international markets can provide geographic

diversification, reducing reliance on the performance of a single country's economy.

Risk Management:

Risk management entails identifying, assessing, and mitigating potential risks that may adversely impact an investment portfolio. Effective risk management involves understanding different types of risks, implementing strategies to manage them, and aligning risk exposure with an investor's objectives and risk tolerance.

Types of Risks:

1. Market Risk: The risk of losses due to movements in the overall market, often measured by factors such as beta and volatility.

2. Credit Risk: The risk of default by borrowers or issuers of debt securities,

leading to potential loss of principal or interest.

3. Liquidity Risk: The risk of not being able to sell an asset quickly at its fair market value, potentially resulting in losses or missed investment opportunities.

4. Inflation Risk: The risk that the purchasing power of investment returns will be eroded by inflation over time.

Risk Management Strategies:

1. Asset Allocation: Determining the appropriate mix of asset classes based on risk tolerance, time horizon, and financial goals.

2. Diversification: As discussed earlier, diversification is a powerful risk management tool that can help spread risk across different investments.

3. Use of Derivatives and Hedging: Investors can use derivatives such as options and

futures to hedge against specific risks in their portfolio.

4. Active Monitoring and Rebalancing: Regularly monitoring the portfolio's performance and rebalancing it to maintain the desired level of diversification and risk exposure.

Diversification and risk management are paramount in the realm of investing, serving as essential tools for building resilient investment portfolios and achieving long-term financial objectives. By strategically diversifying across asset classes, sectors, and geographies, and implementing effective risk management practices, investors can navigate market uncertainties and position themselves for sustainable wealth accumulation. Understanding the intricacies of diversification and risk management empowers investors to make informed decisions, effectively balance risk and reward, and ultimately strengthen their financial well-being.

Understanding compounding interest and its power over time

Understanding compounding interest and its power over time is crucial for anyone seeking to build long-term wealth and achieve financial independence. Compounding interest is a concept that allows an initial sum of money to grow exponentially over time as both the original amount and the interest earned on it continue to earn interest. In this comprehensive discussion, we will explore the mechanics of compounding interest, its impact on investments, and the profound implications it has for individuals' financial futures.

Mechanics of Compounding Interest:

When capital is subjected to compounding interest, the interest earned on the initial principal is reinvested to generate additional interest in subsequent periods. As a result, the overall value of the investment grows at an accelerating rate, leading to a snowball effect of wealth accumulation. The compounding process can occur at different frequencies, such as annually, semi-annually, quarterly, monthly, or even daily, with more frequent compounding leading to faster growth due to the more frequent addition of interest to the principal amount.

Power of Compounding Over Time:

The true power of compounding interest becomes apparent when considering the impact of time on investment growth. Given sufficient time, compounding can lead to significant multiplication of wealth, turning a relatively modest initial investment into a substantial sum over the long term. This phenomenon is often referred to as the "eighth wonder of the world," as it has the potential to transform small, regular contributions into sizeable financial assets.

Factors Affecting Compounding Interest:

1. Principal Amount: The larger the initial investment, the greater the absolute amount of interest earned and reinvested, leading to a larger final value over time.

2. Interest Rate: Higher interest rates result in faster growth through compounding, as more interest accrues on the principal amount.

3. Time Horizon: The longer the time period over which compounding occurs, the more pronounced the effects of compounding interest.

Example of Compounding Interest:

Let's consider an illustrative example with an initial investment of $10,000, an annual interest rate of 5%, and compounding on an annual basis. After the first year, the investment would grow to $10,500, with $500 representing the interest earned. In the second year, the interest would be calculated not only on the original $10,000 but also on the $500 in interest from the previous year, leading to a total of $10,500 + ($10,500 * 5%) = $11,025. This process continues, with each year's interest contributing to the next year's growth, resulting in exponential wealth accumulation over time.

Implications of Compounding Interest:

1. Long-Term Investing: The power of compounding underscores the benefits of long-term investing, emphasizing the

importance of starting early and allowing investments to grow over extended periods.

2. Wealth Preservation: By harnessing the power of compounding, individuals can preserve and grow their wealth, paving the way for financial security and achieving future goals, such as retirement or education funding.

3. Risk Mitigation: Compounding interest can act as a buffer against inflation and other economic forces, helping to maintain the purchasing power of investments over time.

Understanding compounding interest and its power over time is essential for individuals seeking to build and preserve wealth. By recognizing the exponential growth potential of compounding, individuals can make informed investment decisions, set realistic financial goals, and proactively take advantage of the long-term benefits of compounding interest. Embracing the concept of compounding interest empowers individuals to lay the groundwork for enduring financial prosperity and secure their financial well-being for the future.

CHAPTER 4

Real estate and property investment

Real estate and property investment represent a cornerstone of wealth creation and financial security for many individuals and businesses. This form of investment involves the acquisition, ownership, management, rental, and/or sale of real property for the purpose of generating income, building equity, and potentially realizing capital gains. In this comprehensive discussion, we will explore the various aspects of real estate and property investment, including its benefits, different investment strategies, key considerations, and the potential risks and rewards associated with this asset class.

Benefits of Real Estate and Property Investment

1. Income Generation: Real estate can provide a steady stream of passive income through rental payments from tenants, making it an attractive option for investors seeking regular cash flow.

2. Equity Build-Up: Property ownership allows investors to build equity over time as they pay down their mortgage, potentially leading to significant wealth accumulation through property appreciation.

3. Diversification: Real estate offers diversification benefits, as it is considered a distinct asset class that may not move in tandem with traditional financial investments such as stocks and bonds.

4. Hedge Against Inflation: Real estate has historically acted as a hedge against inflation, as property values and rental income tend to

increase in line with or outpace inflationary pressures.

Different Investment Strategies in Real Estate:

1. Rental Properties: Investors can purchase residential or commercial properties and generate income by leasing them to tenants, thereby creating a consistent income stream and potential tax benefits.

2. Flipping Properties: This strategy involves purchasing undervalued properties, renovating or improving them, and then selling them at a higher price to realize a profit. Flipping requires a keen understanding of market dynamics and renovation costs.

3. Real Estate Investment Trusts (REITs): REITs are companies that own, operate, or finance income-generating real estate across

a range of property sectors. Investing in REITs provides exposure to real estate with the added liquidity of a publicly traded security.

Key Considerations for Real Estate Investment:

1. Location: The adage "location, location, location" holds true in real estate investing. A property's location significantly influences its desirability, rental potential, and long-term value appreciation.

2. Market Analysis: Understanding local market dynamics, such as supply and demand trends, rental yields, and potential for property appreciation, is essential for making informed investment decisions.

3. Financing and Leverage: Real estate investments often involve significant capital outlays, and investors commonly use financing to amplify their purchasing power.

Careful consideration of leverage and the associated risks is crucial.

4. Property Management: For rental properties, effective property management is critical to tenant satisfaction, rent collection, maintenance, and compliance with regulations.

Potential Risks and Rewards:

1. Rewards: Successful real estate investments offer the potential for ongoing rental income, property appreciation, tax benefits, and the opportunity to leverage other people's money through financing.

2. Risks: Real estate investments carry risks such as vacancies, property damage, interest rate fluctuations, regulatory changes, and market volatility, which can impact returns and overall investment performance.

In conclusion, real estate and property investment encompass a diverse array of opportunities for individuals and businesses to build wealth, generate income, and achieve long-term financial objectives. By understanding the benefits, various investment strategies, key considerations, and potential risks and rewards associated with real estate investing, individuals can make informed decisions, mitigate risks, and capitalize on the wealth-building potential of this asset class. Whether pursuing rental properties, property flipping, or REIT investments, a well-executed real estate investment strategy can serve as a valuable component of a diversified investment portfolio and contribute to sustained financial prosperity.

Exploring different types of real estate investments

Real estate investment offers a wide range of opportunities, each with its unique characteristics, benefits, and considerations. In this discussion, we will explore the different types of real estate investments, including residential properties, commercial properties, industrial properties, retail properties, and mixed-use properties.

1. Residential Properties:

   - Single-Family Homes: Investing in single-family homes involves purchasing properties intended for a single family to live in. These can be lucrative as rental properties, offering steady income and potential for appreciation.

- Multi-Family Homes: Multi-family properties encompass duplexes, triplexes, and apartment buildings. Investors can generate multiple streams of income from tenants residing in different units within the same property.

2. Commercial Properties:

- Office Buildings: Investing in office buildings can provide stable long-term income from leasing space to businesses and professionals. Location and demand for office space are critical factors in assessing investment potential.

- Retail Centers: Retail properties include shopping malls, strip malls, and standalone retail spaces. Income is derived from renting space to retail businesses, and success often depends on factors such as foot traffic, tenant mix, and consumer trends.

- Hotels and Hospitality: Hospitality properties cater to travelers and tourists, providing revenue through room rentals, food and beverage services, and event hosting. They are typically influenced by tourism trends and local economic conditions.

3. Industrial Properties:

- Warehouses: Warehouses and distribution centers are essential components of logistics and supply chain operations. Investment in industrial properties can offer stable income from long-term leases to businesses requiring storage and distribution facilities.

- Manufacturing Facilities: Investing in manufacturing facilities involves owning properties used for industrial production. Factors like proximity to transportation networks and availability of skilled labor can impact the suitability of these investments.

4. Retail Properties:

- Shopping Centers: Shopping centers house a variety of retail stores and restaurants, offering income from lease agreements with retail tenants. Their success is closely tied to consumer spending habits and overall economic conditions.

- Stand-Alone Retail: This category includes standalone retail properties leased to individual businesses. Location, visibility, and surrounding demographics are crucial factors influencing the performance of these investments.

5. Mixed-Use Properties:

- Mixed-Use Developments: These properties feature a combination of residential, commercial, and sometimes industrial spaces in the same development. They offer diversification and potential for multiple income streams.

- Live-Work Spaces: Live-work spaces combine residential and commercial elements, allowing individuals to both live and operate a business within the same property.

Key Considerations for Different Types of Real Estate Investments:

- Market Dynamics: Understanding local supply and demand dynamics, demographic trends, and economic indicators is vital for assessing the viability of different real estate investments.

- Risk Profile: Each type of real estate investment carries its own set of risks, such as tenant turnover, market saturation, regulatory changes, and economic downturns. Assessing risk and implementing risk management strategies is crucial.

- Management Requirements: Different types of real estate investments have varying management needs, such as tenant relations, property maintenance, and compliance with regulations. Investors should consider the time and resources required for effective management.

In conclusion, exploring different types of real estate investments offers investors a multitude of avenues to build wealth, generate income, and diversify their investment portfolios. Each type of real estate investment presents distinct opportunities and challenges, requiring careful evaluation of market conditions, risk assessment, and management considerations. By understanding the features, benefits, and key considerations associated with residential, commercial, industrial, retail, and mixed-use properties, investors can make informed decisions to capitalize on the wealth-building potential of real estate. Whether pursuing single-family rentals, office buildings, warehouses, or mixed-use developments, a well-rounded understanding of the nuances of each type of real estate investment can enhance investment success and contribute to long-term financial prosperity.

Understanding property values and market trends

Understanding property values and market trends is essential for anyone involved in real estate, whether as an investor, homeowner, or industry professional. This knowledge allows individuals to make informed decisions about buying, selling, renting, or developing properties. In this detailed exploration, we will delve into the various factors that influence property values and market trends.

1. Location:

- Location is one of the most influential factors in determining property values. Desirable locations with good schools, access to amenities, low crime rates, and proximity to employment centers typically command higher property values.

2. Economic Indicators:

- Local and national economic conditions play a significant role in property values. Factors such as employment rates, job growth, income levels, and overall economic stability impact housing demand and affordability.

3. Demographics:

- Understanding the demographic composition of an area is crucial. Population trends, age distribution, household sizes, and cultural diversity can influence housing preferences and demand for certain types of properties.

4. Supply and Demand Dynamics:

- The balance between housing supply and demand directly affects property values. Low inventory and high demand can lead to price appreciation, while oversupply may result in reduced property values.

5. Property Characteristics:

- Specific attributes of a property, such as size, condition, layout, and architectural style, contribute to its value. Renovated and well-maintained properties typically command higher prices.

6. Market Conditions:

- Understanding the current state of the real estate market is critical. Factors such as interest rates, mortgage availability, and investor sentiment can influence buyer behavior and property values.

7. Zoning and Land Use Regulations:

- Zoning laws, land use restrictions, and development regulations can impact property values by influencing the supply and type of properties allowed in certain areas.

8. Infrastructure and Development Projects:

- The presence of infrastructure projects, transportation improvements, and planned developments can enhance property values in surrounding areas by increasing convenience and desirability.

Market Trends:

1. Appreciation Rates:

- Monitoring property appreciation rates over time provides insights into market trends. This data helps identify areas experiencing rapid appreciation or potential declines in property values.

2. Housing Affordability:

- Assessing housing affordability metrics enables understanding of whether property values align with local income levels. High affordability can support sustained demand and price stability.

3. Rental Market Dynamics:

- Rental market trends, such as vacancy rates, rental yields, and tenant preferences, can offer valuable insights into property investment opportunities and potential rental income.

4. Technology and Innovation:

- Technological advancements and innovative urban planning can influence market trends, shaping the demand for smart homes, sustainable properties, and mixed-use developments.

5. External Factors:

- External factors, including geopolitical events, changes in government policies, and global economic shifts, can impact property values and market conditions.

Analyzing and Utilizing Data:

- Access to reliable data sources, including real estate market reports, housing market indices, and local economic indicators, is essential for assessing property values and market trends.

Applying the Knowledge:

- Armed with an understanding of property values and market trends, individuals can make informed decisions about buying, selling, financing, or investing in real estate. This knowledge also aids in property valuation, negotiation, and risk management strategies.

Understanding property values and market trends requires a comprehensive analysis of numerous interconnected factors, ranging from location and economic indicators to market conditions and demographic trends. By delving deep into these influences, individuals can gain valuable insights into the dynamic nature of real estate markets, empowering them to make informed decisions and navigate the nuances of property valuation and investment in an ever-changing real estate landscape

Tips for successful property management and rental income generation

Successfully managing rental properties and generating a steady rental income involves various strategies, from property maintenance to tenant relations and financial management. Here, we will explore comprehensive tips for achieving success in property management and maximizing rental income generation.

1. Property Maintenance and Upkeep:

- Regular maintenance and timely repairs are crucial for preserving the value of rental properties. Establishing a proactive maintenance schedule and promptly addressing any issues can minimize costly repairs and ensure tenant satisfaction.

2. Tenant Screening and Selection:

- Implement a thorough tenant screening process to identify reliable and financially stable tenants. Conducting background checks, verifying employment and rental history, and checking credit scores can help in selecting tenants who are likely to fulfill lease agreements and maintain the property well.

3. Lease Agreements and Legal Compliance:

- Craft clear and comprehensive lease agreements that outline tenant responsibilities, rental terms, and property rules. Adhering to local landlord-tenant laws and staying informed about legal requirements is essential for avoiding disputes and ensuring legal compliance.

4. Effective Communication with Tenants:

- Maintaining open lines of communication with tenants fosters a positive landlord-tenant relationship. Promptly addressing tenant inquiries, providing advance notice for property inspections or renovations, and keeping tenants informed about any changes or developments can contribute to tenant satisfaction and retention.

5. Rental Pricing and Market Analysis:

- Conduct thorough market research to determine competitive rental rates in the area. Understanding local market trends and property demand enables setting appropriate rental prices to attract tenants while maximizing rental income.

6. Marketing and Tenant Acquisition:

- Utilize effective marketing strategies to attract potential tenants. Employing online listing platforms, professional photography, and compelling property descriptions can help in showcasing rental properties and reaching a wide audience of prospective tenants.

7. Financial Management and Budgeting:

- Develop a detailed financial plan for managing rental income and expenses. Tracking income, budgeting for maintenance and operating costs, and establishing a contingency fund for unexpected expenses are essential for maintaining financial stability and profitability.

8. Efficient Property Management Tools and Resources:

- Leveraging technology and property management software can streamline administrative tasks, rent collection, maintenance requests, and financial reporting. Utilizing these tools can enhance operational efficiency and organization.

9. Regular Property Inspections and Preventive Measures:

- Conduct periodic property inspections to assess the condition of the rental units and identify any maintenance needs. Implement preventive measures to minimize potential risks and ensure the safety and well-being of tenants.

10. Flexibility and Adaptability:

- Remain flexible and adaptable in addressing evolving market conditions and tenant needs. Being responsive to changing rental market dynamics and willing to make adjustments based on feedback can contribute to long-term success in property management.

Maximizing Rental Income:

1. Value-Add Improvements:

   - Identify opportunities for value-add improvements that can increase the desirability and rental value of the property. Renovations, energy-efficient upgrades, and amenities enhancements can lead to higher rental income potential.

2. Tenant Retention Strategies:

   - Implement initiatives to enhance tenant satisfaction and encourage lease renewals. Providing quality customer service, addressing tenant concerns promptly, and offering incentives for lease extensions can contribute to stable rental income.

3. Opportunistic Rental Pricing:

- Take advantage of favorable market conditions to adjust rental prices when warranted. Strategic timing for rental increases and lease negotiations can optimize rental income without compromising tenant retention.

4. Diversification and Portfolio Expansion:

- Consider expanding the rental property portfolio to diversify income streams and capitalize on investment opportunities in growing markets. Acquiring additional properties with strong rental potential can contribute to long-term income growth.

5. Strong Financial Management:

- Prudent financial planning, including optimizing rental property financing, refinancing opportunities, and evaluating tax implications, can help maximize rental income and overall investment returns.

Successful property management and rental income generation require a multifaceted approach, encompassing diligent property maintenance, tenant-focused strategies, and financial acumen. By implementing the aforementioned tips and consistently adapting to market dynamics, property owners and managers can position themselves for sustained success in the rental property market.**

CHAPTER 5

Entrepreneurship and Business Ventures

Entrepreneurship refers to the process of conceptualizing, developing, and managing a business venture with the aim of creating innovative solutions, generating value, and assuming the associated financial risks. Business ventures encompass the initiatives undertaken by entrepreneurs to establish or expand commercial enterprises, often driven by a vision for growth and sustainability.

Key Components and Concepts:

1. Innovation and Creativity: Entrepreneurship involves the cultivation of innovative ideas and the ability to envision new products, services, or business models

that address unmet needs or create superior value in the market. Creative thinking and problem-solving are vital components of successful entrepreneurship.

2. Risk-Taking and Opportunity Recognition: Entrepreneurs are willing to take calculated risks in pursuit of opportunities. They possess the acumen to identify gaps in the market, anticipate consumer demands, and capitalize on emerging trends, leveraging these insights to shape their business ventures.

3. Business Planning and Strategy: Effective entrepreneurship entails strategic planning, where entrepreneurs develop comprehensive business plans, outline their objectives, and devise strategies for achieving sustainable growth. This includes considerations such as target markets, competitive positioning, marketing approaches, and operational frameworks.

4. Resource Mobilization and Management: Entrepreneurs must secure and manage resources, including financial capital, human talent, and operational assets, to drive the success of their business ventures. Resource optimization and efficient management are critical for long-term viability.

5. Adaptability and Resilience: Entrepreneurs operate in dynamic environments and must exhibit adaptability in response to market fluctuations, technological advancements, and changing consumer preferences. Resilience, the ability to overcome setbacks and learn from failures, is a fundamental trait of successful entrepreneurs.

6. Market Analysis and Customer Focus: Understanding market dynamics and consumer behavior is essential for effective entrepreneurship. Entrepreneurs conduct market research, assess competitive landscapes, and prioritize customer-centric

approaches to product development and service delivery.

7. Legal and Regulatory Considerations: Entrepreneurs must navigate legal and regulatory frameworks governing business operations, intellectual property rights, taxation, and compliance. Understanding and adhering to these requirements is integral to the sustainability of business ventures.

Significance and Impact:

Entrepreneurship and business ventures play a pivotal role in driving economic growth, fostering innovation, and creating employment opportunities. By introducing new products, services, and business models, entrepreneurs contribute to market dynamism and societal progress. Additionally, successful business ventures can spur wealth creation, inspire industry disruptions, and serve as catalysts for positive societal change.

Challenges and Opportunities:

While entrepreneurship offers opportunities for personal fulfillment and financial rewards, it also presents inherent challenges, including financial uncertainties, market competition, operational complexities, and regulatory hurdles. Nonetheless, proactive entrepreneurship can lead to the establishment of successful enterprises and the realization of entrepreneurial visions.

In summary, entrepreneurship and business ventures embody the spirit of initiative, innovation, and risk-taking, serving as engines of economic vitality and transformative change. By embracing creativity, resilience, and strategic vision, entrepreneurs can envision, establish, and sustain business ventures that drive progress and prosperity in diverse industries and societal contexts.

Evaluating potential business opportunities

Evaluating potential business opportunities is a critical process that involves assessing various aspects of a proposed venture to determine its viability, feasibility, and potential for success. Here's a detailed exploration of the topic:

Identifying Market Needs and Trends:

One of the initial steps in evaluating business opportunities is conducting market research to identify unmet needs, emerging trends, and consumer preferences. This involves analyzing demographic data, consumer behavior, and industry reports to gain insights into market gaps and potential demand for new products or services.

Assessing Competitive Landscape:

Understanding existing competitors and their strengths and weaknesses is essential. A thorough analysis of the competitive landscape helps in identifying opportunities for differentiation, niche positioning, and the potential challenges the new venture may face in the market.

Financial Considerations:

An in-depth evaluation of the financial aspects of the business opportunity is crucial. This includes estimating start-up costs, projecting revenue streams, analyzing profit margins, and assessing potential return on investment. Financial feasibility studies help in determining the financial sustainability and attractiveness of the opportunity.

Technical and Operational Feasibility:

Assessing the technical requirements and operational considerations of the proposed business opportunity is necessary to ensure that the venture can be effectively executed. This may include evaluating the availability of necessary resources, technological infrastructure, and operational capabilities.

Regulatory and Legal Assessment:

Understanding the regulatory environment and legal considerations related to the industry and location is vital. Compliance with licensing requirements, industry regulations, and legal frameworks is essential for mitigating risks and ensuring the legality of the business operations.

SWOT Analysis:

Conducting a comprehensive SWOT (Strengths, Weaknesses, Opportunities, Threats) analysis aids in evaluating the internal and external factors that can influence the success of the business opportunity. This analysis helps in identifying areas of strength to leverage, weaknesses to address, potential opportunities to pursue, and threats to mitigate.

Assessing Resource Availability:

Evaluating the availability of human capital, expertise, and other resources necessary to execute the business opportunity is important. Understanding the capacity to acquire, manage, and optimize resources is integral to the feasibility assessment.

Scalability and Growth Potential:

Assessing the scalability and growth potential of the business opportunity is crucial for long-term success. Evaluating potential expansion avenues, market scalability, and adaptability to changing market dynamics helps in understanding the future prospects of the venture.

Risk Analysis and Contingency Planning:

Identifying and analyzing potential risks associated with the business opportunity is essential. Developing contingency plans to address possible challenges and mitigate risks supports prudent decision-making.

Evaluating potential business opportunities requires a comprehensive and systematic approach that encompasses market analysis, financial assessments, technical evaluations, legal considerations, and risk analysis. By rigorously evaluating these facets, entrepreneurs and business professionals can make informed decisions about pursuing or investing in viable and promising business opportunities.

Strategies for funding and scaling a business

The strategies for funding and scaling a business are essential in driving its growth and expansion. Here's a thorough exploration of the topic:

1. Bootstrapping:

Bootstrapping involves self-funding a business using personal savings, revenues generated by the business, or operating with minimal external capital. This strategy allows founders to maintain control and ownership of the business while focusing on organic growth. Bootstrapping also demonstrates financial discipline and resourcefulness, which can be attractive to potential investors in the future.

2. Angel Investors:

Angel investors are individuals who provide capital for start-up businesses in exchange for ownership equity or convertible debt. These investors often bring valuable expertise, mentorship, and networks, in addition to funding. Engaging with angel investors can provide early-stage financing and strategic guidance for scaling the business.

3. Venture Capital:

Venture capital firms invest in high-potential start-ups and early-stage companies in exchange for equity. Venture capital funding can fuel rapid scaling by providing substantial financial backing, strategic support, and industry connections. However, it often involves giving up a significant portion of ownership and requires meeting rigorous growth targets.

4. Crowdfunding:

Crowdfunding platforms enable entrepreneurs to raise funds from a large number of individuals, often in exchange for rewards, pre-sales of products, or equity. Crowdfunding can be an effective strategy for validating market demand, securing initial capital, and engaging with a community of supporters who can contribute to the scaling of the business.

5. Strategic Partnerships:

Forming strategic partnerships with other businesses, industry players, or investors can provide access to resources, capital, distribution channels, and expertise that facilitate scaling. By aligning with partners who share complementary goals and capabilities, businesses can leverage synergies to accelerate growth and expansion.

6. Debt Financing:

Utilizing debt financing through loans, lines of credit, or small business administration (SBA) loans can provide access to capital for scaling operations, investing in infrastructure, and expanding the business. While debt financing involves repayment obligations, it allows businesses to retain ownership and control without diluting equity.

7. Accelerator and Incubator Programs:

Participating in accelerator or incubator programs can provide start-ups with funding, mentorship, training, and networking opportunities to accelerate growth. These programs often offer access to investors, industry experts, and resources that can support the scaling of the business in a structured and supportive environment.

8. Mezzanine Financing:

Mezzanine financing involves raising capital through a combination of debt and equity, often at a later stage of business maturity. This form of financing can provide flexible capital for scaling initiatives, such as expansion into new markets, product development, or strategic acquisitions, while preserving equity ownership.

Scaling Strategies:

In addition to funding, implementing effective scaling strategies is essential for sustainable growth. These may include expanding into new markets, diversifying product offerings, optimizing operational efficiency, investing in marketing and sales, enhancing customer retention and loyalty programs, and leveraging technology for automation and innovation.

The strategies for funding and scaling a business encompass various sources of capital, including bootstrapping, external investors, strategic partnerships, and alternative financing options. By combining sound funding strategies with effective scaling initiatives, businesses can fuel their growth, expand their market presence, and achieve long-term success.

Managing risks and challenges associated with entrepreneurship

Managing risks and challenges is a fundamental aspect of entrepreneurship, as it directly impacts the success and sustainability of a business. Here's a thorough exploration of the topic:

1. Understanding Risks and Challenges:

- Market Risks: These include changes in consumer preferences, market competition, and economic downturns that can affect demand for products or services.

- Financial Risks: Entrepreneurs face challenges related to cash flow management, securing funding, and managing financial obligations.

- Operational Risks: This encompasses issues such as supply chain disruptions, production inefficiencies, and regulatory compliance.

- Strategic Risks: Making incorrect strategic decisions, encountering unexpected disruptions, or facing technological obsolescence are examples of strategic risks.

2. Risk Management Strategies:

- Risk Identification: Thoroughly analyzing potential risks and their impact on the business is crucial. This involves conducting risk assessments, scenario planning, and utilizing tools such as SWOT analysis.

- Risk Mitigation: Implementing strategies to reduce the impact of risks, such as diversifying product lines, building strong supplier relationships, and developing contingency plans for potential disruptions.

- Risk Transfer: Utilizing methods such as insurance, outsourcing certain functions, or forming strategic partnerships to share or transfer risks to other parties.

3. Financial Challenges:

- Cash Flow Management: Monitoring cash flow, optimizing payment terms, and managing working capital are essential to address financial challenges.

- Access to Capital: Securing funding through sources such as venture capital, loans, or angel investors can help address financial challenges associated with growth and expansion.

- Cost Control: Implementing cost-effective measures, negotiating vendor contracts, and prioritizing expenses to maintain financial stability during challenging periods.

4. Operational Challenges:

- Supply Chain Management: Ensuring a resilient and efficient supply chain through diversification, inventory management, and risk assessment to mitigate disruptions.

- Regulatory Compliance: Staying abreast of legal and regulatory requirements to minimize the risks associated with non-compliance and potential penalties.

- Talent Acquisition and Retention: Building a skilled and motivated team through effective recruitment, training, and retention strategies to address operational challenges.

5. Uncertainty and Adaptability:

- Entrepreneurs must navigate uncertainty and be adaptable in response to unforeseen challenges by fostering a culture of innovation, agility, and continuous learning within their organizations.

- Embracing flexibility and being open to pivoting business models, product offerings, or strategies in response to changing market conditions and customer needs is crucial.

6. Psychological Resilience:

- The entrepreneurial journey often involves psychological challenges such as stress, anxiety, and self-doubt. Building resilience, seeking support from mentors or peers, and prioritizing mental well-being are essential for managing these challenges effectively.

Managing risks and challenges associated with entrepreneurship requires a comprehensive understanding of potential threats, proactive risk management strategies, financial prudence, operational excellence, adaptability, and resilience. By addressing these aspects effectively, entrepreneurs can navigate uncertainties and position their businesses for long-term success and sustainable growth.

CHAPTER 6

Retirement planning and wealth preservation

Retirement planning involves the process of setting financial goals and taking steps to achieve financial security for one's retirement years. It includes strategies such as choosing appropriate investment vehicles, building a retirement nest egg through regular savings, and optimizing sources of retirement income such as Social Security benefits and pension plans.

Wealth preservation, on the other hand, refers to managing and safeguarding accumulated assets to maintain and protect one's financial worth over time. This may involve diversifying investments, managing risks through insurance and estate planning, and making informed financial decisions in order to sustain and potentially grow one's wealth.

In essence, retirement planning focuses on preparing for a financially secure retirement, while wealth preservation centers around safeguarding and managing accumulated assets to maintain long-term financial stability and potentially pass on wealth to future generations. Both are critical components of a comprehensive financial plan aimed at ensuring financial security throughout one's lifetime and beyond.

Navigating retirement accounts and investment options

Navigating retirement accounts and investment options can be an important aspect of financial planning as you prepare for retirement. Retirement accounts, such as 401(k) plans, IRAs (Individual Retirement Accounts), and Roth IRAs, offer tax advantages and are designed to help individuals save for retirement. It's important to understand the different types of retirement accounts available to you and the investment options within these accounts.

When it comes to retirement accounts, there are a few key considerations to keep in mind:

1. Types of retirement accounts: There are various types of retirement accounts, including employer-sponsored plans like 401(k)s and 403(b)s, as well as individual retirement accounts such as Traditional IRAs and Roth IRAs. Each type of account has its own eligibility criteria, contribution limits, and tax benefits.

2. Tax implications: Understanding the tax implications of different retirement accounts is crucial. For example, contributions to traditional 401(k)s and IRAs are typically tax-deductible, while withdrawals in retirement are taxed as ordinary income. On the other hand, Roth accounts are funded with after-tax dollars, and qualified withdrawals are tax-free.

3. Investment options: Within retirement accounts, individuals have the opportunity to invest in a range of options such as stocks, bonds, mutual funds, and exchange-traded funds (ETFs). It's important to consider your risk tolerance, investment goals, and time horizon when selecting investment options within your retirement accounts.

4. Employer matching: If your employer offers a matching contribution to your retirement account, it's wise to take full advantage of this benefit as it can significantly boost your retirement savings.

In navigating retirement accounts and investment options, it's generally advisable to seek guidance from financial professionals or advisors who can help assess your individual financial situation and provide personalized recommendations. Additionally, educating yourself about the various retirement accounts and investment options available can empower you to make informed decisions that align with your long-term financial goals. Regularly reviewing and adjusting your investment strategy as you progress toward retirement can also be beneficial in optimizing your retirement savings.

Estate planning and legacy wealth management

Estate planning and legacy wealth management are essential components of financial planning that involve preparing for the transfer of assets and wealth to future generations, as well as ensuring that your wishes are carried out in the event of death or incapacity.

Estate Planning:

Estate planning involves the preparation of legal documents and strategies to facilitate the transfer of assets and wealth to heirs and beneficiaries. Key elements of estate planning include:

1. Wills and Trusts: A will is a legal document that outlines how your assets should be distributed upon your death. Trusts can also be used to manage and distribute assets, often providing greater control and flexibility.

2. Power of Attorney and Healthcare Directives: These documents appoint individuals to make financial and medical decisions on your behalf if you become incapacitated.

3. Beneficiary Designations: Ensuring that beneficiary designations on assets like retirement accounts and life insurance policies are up to date and aligned with your overall estate plan.

Legacy Wealth Management:

Legacy wealth management focuses on preserving and potentially growing wealth for future generations while also considering philanthropic or charitable giving. Key considerations in legacy wealth management include:

1.   Wealth Transfer Strategies: Implementation of strategies to minimize estate taxes and ensure an efficient transfer of assets to beneficiaries.

2. Charitable Giving: Developing a plan for philanthropic giving, which may include establishing a charitable foundation, donor-advised fund, or including charitable bequests in your estate plan.

3. Family Governance and Education: Establishing structures and processes to educate and prepare future generations to responsibly manage inherited wealth, often involving family meetings and financial education programs.

4.   Intergenerational   Communication: Facilitating open and clear communication among family members about wealth, values, and expectations to promote family unity and understanding.

Seeking Professional Guidance:

Given the complexities and legal implications involved in estate planning and legacy wealth management, it's advisable to work with experienced estate planning attorneys, financial planners, and tax professionals. These professionals can help you navigate the various options and legal requirements, and tailor a plan that aligns with your specific goals and values.

In conclusion, estate planning and legacy wealth management are crucial aspects of comprehensive financial planning. Through careful preparation and professional guidance, individuals can create a legacy that effectively manages and passes on their wealth in a manner that reflects their values and long-term objectives.

Maximizing financial security in later years

Maximizing financial security in later years is a critical aspect of personal financial planning, especially as individuals approach retirement and beyond. This involves taking proactive steps to ensure a comfortable and stable financial future, with consideration given to factors such as retirement savings, healthcare costs, and estate planning. Here are some key strategies for maximizing financial security in later years:

1. Retirement Savings:

- Regularly contribute to retirement accounts such as 401(k)s, IRAs, and other tax-advantaged plans to build a substantial nest egg.

- Consider increasing contributions as income grows or taking advantage of catch-up contributions for those aged 50 and older.

- Diversify investments to balance risk and return, adjusting asset allocation over time to align with changing goals and risk tolerance.

2. Social Security Planning:

- Understand the implications of when to start claiming Social Security benefits. Delaying benefits can result in higher monthly payments.

- Consider spousal and survivor benefits in Social Security claiming strategies to maximize household income over the long term.

3. Healthcare and Long-Term Care:

- Plan for healthcare expenses in retirement, including Medicare premiums, co-pays, and potential long-term care costs.

- Consider purchasing long-term care insurance, or explore other options to protect against the potential financial impact of chronic illness or disability.

4. Estate Planning:

- Establish or update a comprehensive estate plan that includes wills, trusts, and powers of attorney to protect assets and provide for loved ones.

- Consider gifting strategies and charitable giving as part of an overall estate plan, while understanding the tax implications.

5. Budgeting and Cash Flow Management:

- Create a realistic budget for retirement that accounts for living expenses, travel, healthcare, and leisure activities.

- Monitor cash flow and investment income to ensure sustainable withdrawals from retirement accounts and other sources.

6. Financial Education and Professional Advice:

- Stay informed about changes in financial markets, tax laws, and retirement planning strategies.

- Seek guidance from financial advisors and planners to develop a customized plan that addresses individual financial goals and concerns.

By proactively addressing these areas of financial planning, individuals can work towards achieving greater financial security and peace of mind in their later years. It's important to regularly review and adjust financial plans to reflect changing circumstances, market conditions, and personal goals, ensuring that financial security is maintained throughout retirement and beyond.

CHAPTER 7

Advanced Wealth-Building Tactics

Advanced wealth-building tactics involve sophisticated strategies and approaches to grow and protect assets, optimize investment returns, minimize taxes, and maximize long-term financial security. These tactics are typically suited for individuals with a substantial net worth and a strong understanding of financial markets and planning. Here are some advanced wealth-building tactics along with explanations:

Tax planning and optimization strategies

Tax planning and optimization strategies are essential components of overall financial management, aimed at minimizing tax liabilities, maximizing after-tax returns, and optimizing long-term wealth accumulation. These strategies involve a comprehensive approach to structuring investments, income, and expenses in a tax-efficient manner while complying with existing tax laws and regulations. Below are some in-depth explanations of tax planning and optimization strategies:

1. Asset Location:

- Asset location involves strategically placing assets in different types of accounts to minimize overall tax liability. For example, holding tax-efficient investments such as stocks in taxable brokerage accounts and tax-inefficient investments such as bonds in tax-advantaged retirement accounts can help optimize after-tax returns.

- By considering the tax treatment of various investment vehicles and aligning them with the most appropriate account types, individuals can enhance the tax efficiency of their investment portfolios.

2. Tax-Loss Harvesting:

- Tax-loss harvesting involves strategically selling investments that have experienced a loss to offset capital gains and reduce taxable income. By realizing losses, investors can use them to offset realized gains, thereby lowering their overall tax bill.

- Additionally, harvested losses can be carried forward to future tax years to offset gains or up to a certain amount of ordinary income, providing potential tax benefits in the long term.

3. Retirement Account Strategies:

- Maximizing contributions to tax-advantaged retirement accounts, such as 401(k)s, IRAs, and Roth IRAs, can offer significant tax benefits. Contributions to these accounts can reduce current taxable income, allow for tax-deferred growth, or provide tax-free withdrawals in the case of Roth accounts.

- Implementing conversion strategies, such as Roth IRA conversions or backdoor Roth contributions, can also be used to optimize tax outcomes and provide greater flexibility in retirement income planning.

4. Charitable Giving and Donor-Advised Funds:

- Utilizing charitable giving strategies, including donating appreciated assets or establishing donor-advised funds, can result in tax deductions while supporting charitable causes.

- Contributing appreciated securities or other assets directly to charitable organizations can help avoid capital gains taxes on the appreciation while allowing for a charitable deduction based on the fair market value of the donated assets.

5. Tax-Efficient Investment Vehicles:

- Investing in tax-efficient vehicles, such as municipal bonds, exchange-traded funds (ETFs) with low turnover, and index funds, can help minimize tax exposure on investment income and capital gains.

- By carefully selecting investments with consideration for their tax implications, investors can optimize after-tax returns and reduce their overall tax burden.

6. Estate and Gift Tax Planning:

- Proactive estate planning, including the use of trusts, gifting strategies, and leveraging estate tax exemptions, can help minimize estate taxes and preserve wealth for future generations.

- Structuring estate plans to take advantage of stepped-up basis provisions and utilizing tools such as family limited partnerships can contribute to efficient transfer of assets with minimized tax consequences.

7. Business and Income Deferral Strategies:

- Business owners and self-employed individuals can benefit from income deferral strategies, such as deferring compensation, utilizing retirement plans, and timing business income recognition to manage their tax liabilities.

- Structuring income and expenses to align with tax brackets and taking advantage of available deductions, credits, and incentives can further optimize tax outcomes.

It's important to emphasize that tax planning and optimization strategies should be implemented within the broader context of an individual's financial goals, risk tolerance, and overall wealth management plan. Additionally, given the complexity of tax laws and regulations, consulting with qualified tax advisors, financial planners, and legal professionals is crucial to ensure that these strategies are tailored to specific circumstances and comply with applicable tax laws. Staying informed about changes in tax legislation and seeking professional guidance as needed are essential components of effective tax planning and optimization.

Exploring alternative investments (venture capital, private equity, etc.)

Exploring alternative investments, such as venture capital and private equity, involves delving into non-traditional asset classes that offer potential for higher returns but also entail increased risk and complexity. These investments typically involve placing capital in non-publicly traded securities, often with longer investment horizons and less liquidity compared to traditional stocks and bonds. Here's a detailed explanation of some key alternative investment options:

1. Venture Capital (VC):

- Venture capital involves investing in early-stage or growth-stage companies with substantial growth potential. VC investors provide funding to startups and high-growth businesses in exchange for an ownership stake.

- This form of investment offers the potential for substantial capital appreciation if the invested companies succeed and achieve significant growth or exit through acquisitions or initial public offerings (IPOs).

- Due diligence in venture capital entails assessing business models, market potential, management teams, and competitive landscapes to identify promising opportunities and manage risk.

2. Private Equity (PE):

- Private equity involves investing in privately held companies, often with the goal of restructuring, expanding, or improving the operational efficiency of these businesses to drive value creation.

- PE investors may acquire controlling stakes in mature companies, execute buyouts, or participate in growth equity investments to support expansion plans and strategic initiatives.

- The return potential in private equity stems from enhancing the performance of portfolio companies and realizing gains upon exit events, such as selling to strategic buyers or conducting secondary buyouts.

3. Hedge Funds:

- Hedge funds are pooled investment vehicles that employ various strategies, including long/short equity, event-driven, global macro, and relative value, to generate returns irrespective of market direction.

- These funds often pursue complex or specialized investment approaches, such as leveraging derivatives, arbitrage, and alternative asset classes, seeking to deliver absolute returns while managing risk exposures.

- Hedge fund investments may offer diversification benefits and distinct return drivers compared to traditional stocks and bonds, but they typically come with higher fees and less transparency.

4. Real Assets:

- Real assets encompass tangible investments such as real estate, commodities, infrastructure, and natural resources, offering potential inflation protection and income generation.

- Investing in real estate can involve owning properties directly, participating in real estate investment trusts (REITs), or investing in private real estate funds focused on development, income-producing assets, or distressed opportunities.

- Infrastructure investments encompass assets like toll roads, airports, utilities, and renewable energy projects, providing long-term cash flows and exposure to essential services and economic development.

5. Distressed Debt:

- Distressed debt investing involves purchasing the debt of financially troubled companies or distressed securities at discounts, with the expectation of participating in restructurings or turnarounds.

- Investors in distressed debt seek to capitalize on potential value recovery and restructuring outcomes, often by assuming control or influencing corporate reorganizations and debt-to-equity conversions.

- This alternative investment strategy provides opportunities to benefit from market inefficiencies and distressed situations, requiring specialized credit analysis and legal expertise.

It's important to note that alternative investments often have unique characteristics, including illiquidity, complex valuation methodologies, and varying regulatory considerations. Additionally, due diligence, manager selection, and ongoing monitoring are critical factors when considering these investments, emphasizing the need for thorough research and risk assessment.

Investors should also consider their risk tolerance, time horizon, and portfolio diversification requirements when incorporating alternative investments into their overall asset allocation. Given the complexities involved, seeking guidance from experienced financial advisors, investment professionals, and legal or tax advisors is advisable before committing capital to alternative investment strategies. Furthermore, staying informed about regulatory developments, market dynamics, and evolving best practices is essential for effectively navigating the landscape of alternative investments.

Wealth preservation and wealth transfer strategies

Wealth preservation and wealth transfer strategies are essential components of comprehensive financial planning, particularly for individuals and families with substantial assets. These strategies aim to protect and sustain wealth across generations, address estate planning considerations, minimize tax impact, and facilitate the smooth transfer of assets to heirs or beneficiaries. Here's a detailed exploration of wealth preservation and transfer strategies:

Wealth Preservation Strategies:

1. Diversification and Asset Allocation:

- Diversifying investment holdings across various asset classes, such as stocks, bonds, real estate, and alternative investments, helps manage risk and mitigate potential losses during market downturns.

- Strategic asset allocation aims to balance risk and return by aligning investment portfolios with long-term objectives and risk tolerance.

2. Estate Planning:

- Establishing a well-structured estate plan is crucial for protecting wealth and ensuring efficient transfer to intended beneficiaries.

- Utilizing wills, trusts, and beneficiary designations can help manage the distribution of assets, address specific family needs, and potentially reduce estate taxes and probate costs.

3. Insurance Solutions:

- Life insurance policies, particularly whole life and universal life, can serve as wealth preservation tools by providing death benefit proceeds to beneficiaries and accumulating cash value over time.

- Long-term care insurance and disability income insurance are also important considerations to safeguard against potential healthcare and income-related risks.

4. Risk Management and Liability Protection:

- Implementing risk management strategies, such as liability insurance and asset protection trusts, can shield wealth from legal claims, creditor actions, and unforeseen liabilities.

- Structuring ownership of assets and business interests through entities like limited liability companies (LLCs) or family limited partnerships (FLPs) can provide additional safeguards.

5. Tax Planning:

- Engaging in proactive tax planning is critical for preserving wealth, minimizing tax liabilities, and optimizing overall financial efficiency.

- Techniques like gifting, charitable giving, and the use of tax-advantaged accounts and vehicles can help reduce estate taxes, income taxes, and capital gains taxes, thereby preserving more wealth for future generations.

Wealth Transfer Strategies:

1. Trust-Based Planning:

- Establishing revocable or irrevocable trusts, such as living trusts, testamentary trusts, and generation-skipping trusts, allows for the structured transfer of assets while specifying conditions for distribution and providing potential creditor protection.

- Trusts can also facilitate the management of assets for minor or incapacitated beneficiaries and grantors' control over asset disposition posthumously.

2. Lifetime Gifting:

- Utilizing annual gift exclusions, lifetime gift tax exemptions, and direct payments for medical and educational expenses allows individuals to transfer wealth during their lifetimes, reducing the size of their taxable estates.

- Strategic gifting to family members, beneficiaries, and charitable organizations can help accomplish wealth transfer objectives while fostering philanthropic legacies.

3. Business Succession Planning:

- For business owners, implementing a succession plan is vital to effectively transition ownership and management responsibilities to family members, key employees, or external acquirers.

- Techniques like buy-sell agreements, employee stock ownership plans (ESOPs), and family governance structures are common strategies in business succession planning.

4. Legacy and Philanthropy:

- Philanthropic endeavors, including establishing private foundations, donor-advised funds, or charitable trusts, provide opportunities to support charitable causes, engage family members in philanthropy, and leave a lasting societal impact.

- Legacy planning involves documenting family history, values, and intentions, allowing future generations to understand their heritage and maintain continuity of wealth stewardship.

5. Coordination of Legal and Financial Documents:

- Ensuring alignment among wills, trusts, beneficiary designations, powers of attorney, and other legal instruments is critical for avoiding conflicts, ensuring clarity, and accurately reflecting individuals' wishes regarding wealth transfer.

Wealth preservation and transfer strategies necessitate careful consideration of individual circumstances, family dynamics, legal frameworks, and tax implications. Given the complexity of these matters, collaborating with qualified professionals, such as estate planning attorneys, tax advisors, trust officers, and financial planners, is crucial for developing and executing tailored strategies that align with specific goals and values. Moreover, periodic review and adjustment of these strategies are imperative to accommodate changing laws, family dynamics, and financial circumstances, thereby safeguarding wealth across generations and leaving a meaningful legacy.

CHAPTER 8

Cultivating a wealth mindset

Cultivating a wealth mindset involves adopting an empowering and abundance-oriented perspective toward money, prosperity, and financial success. It encompasses developing positive attitudes, beliefs, and behaviors that foster a proactive and resourceful approach to managing finances, pursuing wealth-building opportunities, and achieving long-term financial security. Here's a comprehensive exploration of cultivating a wealth mindset:

1. Self-Awareness and Empowerment:

- Cultivating a wealth mindset begins with self-awareness and recognizing one's attitudes, beliefs, and emotions related to money and wealth.

- Identifying and reframing any limiting beliefs or negative self-talk about money can empower individuals to adopt a more positive and proactive mindset towards wealth accumulation.

2. Goal Setting and Visioning:

- Establishing clear financial goals, both short-term and long-term, helps individuals focus their energy and resources toward wealth-building endeavors.

- Developing a compelling vision of one's desired financial future creates motivation and direction, guiding actions and decisions in line with wealth creation.

3. Financial Education and Continuous Learning:

- Actively seeking knowledge about personal finance, investment principles, and wealth management strategies is fundamental for cultivating a wealth mindset.

- Regularly engaging in financial literacy programs, reading educational materials, and seeking advice from qualified professionals empowers individuals to make informed financial decisions.

4. Positive Money Habits and Discipline:

- Practicing sound money management habits, such as budgeting, saving, investing, and avoiding unnecessary debt, establishes a foundation for financial discipline.

- Cultivating patience, delayed gratification, and strategic decision-making regarding spending and investing contributes to long-term wealth accumulation.

5. Abundance Mentality and Gratitude:

- Embracing an abundance mindset involves recognizing and appreciating the existing wealth and opportunities in one's life, rather than focusing solely on scarcity or lack.

- Cultivating gratitude for current blessings and achievements fosters a positive outlook, reduces stress, and fuels motivation to pursue additional financial success.

6. Risk-Taking and Resilience:

- Developing a healthy relationship with risk and embracing calculated risks is integral to wealth mindset cultivation, as it fosters openness to new opportunities and innovation.

- Building resilience and learning from setbacks or failures in financial endeavors is essential for maintaining confidence and persistence in pursuing wealth goals.

7. Networking and Collaboration:

- Engaging with like-minded individuals, mentors, and advisors who embody a wealth mindset can provide valuable support, inspiration, and guidance.

- Collaborating with others, leveraging collective knowledge, and seeking opportunities for partnerships or joint ventures can enhance wealth-building prospects.

8. Purpose-Driven Wealth Creation:

- Aligning financial pursuits with personal values, passions, and purpose imbues wealth creation with meaning and fulfillment, transcending mere monetary objectives.

- Intentionally integrating philanthropy, social impact, or legacy planning into wealth-building endeavors amplifies the positive impact of financial success.

9. Visualization and Affirmations:

- Utilizing visualization techniques to mentally rehearse and manifest desired financial outcomes reinforces a proactive and confident wealth mindset.

- Incorporating affirmations and positive self-talk related to financial abundance and success can rewire subconscious beliefs and attitudes toward wealth.

10. Adaptability and Continuous Improvement:

- Embracing change, adapting to evolving market conditions, and remaining open to new opportunities is crucial for sustaining a wealth mindset.

- Committing to ongoing self-improvement, skill development, and agility in financial decision-making enhances adaptability and resilience in pursuing wealth goals.

Cultivating a wealth mindset is a transformative journey that integrates psychological, emotional, and behavioral elements with financial acumen and strategy. By consciously embracing a wealth mindset, individuals can empower themselves to overcome limitations, pursue financial aspirations with confidence and resilience, and ultimately realize enduring financial prosperity and fulfillment.

Developing healthy financial habits and attitudes

Developing healthy financial habits and attitudes involves cultivating a positive relationship with money, making informed and responsible financial decisions, and adopting behaviors that align with long-term financial well-being. Here's a detailed exploration of developing healthy financial habits and attitudes:

1. Budgeting and Financial Planning:

- Creating and sticking to a budget is fundamental for developing healthy financial habits. It involves tracking income, expenses, and savings goals to ensure financial stability and progress.

- Financial planning encompasses setting specific financial objectives, such as saving for emergencies, retirement, or major purchases, and creating a roadmap to achieve these goals.

2. Saving and Investing:

- Cultivating a habit of regular saving, whether through automatic transfers to a savings account or employer-sponsored retirement plans, establishes a foundation for financial security.

- Developing an understanding of different investment options and risk levels helps individuals make informed decisions about growing their wealth over time.

3. Debt Management:

- Adopting responsible borrowing practices and managing existing debt effectively is essential for maintaining healthy finances.

- Prioritizing the repayment of high-interest debt, such as credit card balances, while avoiding accumulating new, unnecessary debt supports financial health.

4. Financial Literacy and Education:

- Actively seeking knowledge about personal finance topics, such as budgeting, investing, taxes, and insurance, empowers individuals to make informed financial decisions.

- Formal financial education, through workshops, courses, or self-study, can provide valuable insights into effective money management practices.

5. Delayed Gratification and Mindful Spending:

- Cultivating the discipline of delaying immediate gratification for long-term benefits encourages mindful spending and supports saving for important financial goals.

- Practicing mindfulness in spending decisions, by considering needs versus wants and evaluating the long-term value of purchases, reinforces healthy financial habits.

6. Goal Setting and Visualization:

- Establishing clear financial goals and visualizing the desired outcomes serves as motivation and guidance for developing healthy financial habits and attitudes.

- Regularly revisiting and updating financial goals enables individuals to stay focused and committed to their financial well-being.

7. Embracing Frugality and Smart Consumerism:

- Embracing frugality involves practicing resourcefulness, seeking value in purchases, and avoiding unnecessary expenses without sacrificing quality of life.

- Engaging in smart consumerism, such as researching best deals, comparison shopping, and leveraging discounts and rewards, supports prudent financial habits.

8. Emergency Fund and Risk Management:

- Establishing and regularly contributing to an emergency fund provides a financial safety net for unexpected expenses or income disruptions.

- Mitigating financial risks through appropriate insurance coverage, such as health, life, and property insurance, safeguards against unforeseen financial setbacks.

9. Open Communication and Financial Teamwork:

- Openly communicating about financial matters with family members or partners fosters shared responsibility and accountability for healthy financial habits.

- Collaborating with others on financial goals and strategies can strengthen resolve and provide support in adhering to positive financial attitudes and behaviors.

10. Gratitude and Contentment:

- Cultivating gratitude for existing financial resources, achievements, and opportunities fosters contentment and reduces the impulse for excessive consumption or lifestyle inflation.

- Focusing on non-material sources of fulfillment and joy, such as relationships, experiences, and personal growth, supports a balanced and healthy perspective on wealth and well-being.

Developing healthy financial habits and attitudes requires a combination of discipline, knowledge, self-awareness, and emotional intelligence. By consciously integrating these principles and practices into daily financial decisions, individuals can create a solid foundation for long-term financial stability, growth, and overall well-being.

Overcoming limiting beliefs and embracing abundance

Overcoming limiting beliefs and embracing abundance is a profound journey of self-discovery, personal growth, and transformation. It involves identifying and challenging deeply ingrained negative thought patterns and replacing them with empowering perspectives that open the door to abundance in all areas of life. Here's a comprehensive exploration of this transformative process:

1. Recognizing Limiting Beliefs:

Identifying and acknowledging limiting beliefs is the first step toward overcoming them. These beliefs are often subconscious and can manifest as self-doubt, fears, or negative self-talk. Examples include "I'm not smart enough to achieve my dreams" or "There's never enough money for me to be truly happy."

2. Understanding the Origins of Limiting Beliefs:

Exploring the origins of these beliefs, which may stem from childhood experiences, societal conditioning, or significant life events, provides insight into their underlying causes. Understanding why and how these beliefs developed can help in dismantling their hold on your mindset.

3. Challenging Limiting Beliefs:

Once identified, it's important to challenge these beliefs by questioning their validity and examining the evidence that supports or contradicts them. This process involves introspection and critical thinking to shift the narrative from self-limitation to self-empowerment.

4. Cultivating Self-Awareness:

Developing self-awareness is crucial for recognizing when limiting beliefs surface in daily thoughts and behaviors. Mindfulness practices, journaling, and seeking feedback from trusted individuals can aid in increasing awareness of these patterns.

5. Reframing Perspectives:

Embracing abundance requires transforming limited perspectives into expansive ones. This involves reframing thoughts and beliefs to focus on possibilities, gratitude, and the inherent potential for growth and fulfillment.

6. Practicing Gratitude:

Cultivating a mindset of gratitude serves as a powerful antidote to scarcity thinking. Recognizing and appreciating the abundance already present in one's life fosters a positive outlook and attracts further abundance.

7. Setting Empowering Intentions:

Setting clear, positive intentions aligned with abundance and growth reinforces a mindset of possibility and opportunity. Intention setting directs energy and focus toward constructive pursuits.

8. Self-Compassion and Forgiveness:

Embracing abundance involves releasing self-judgment and embracing self-compassion. Forgiving oneself for past beliefs and behaviors creates space for positive transformation and growth.

9. Surrounding Oneself with Supportive Influences:

Engaging with supportive communities, mentors, or literature that align with an abundance mindset can provide encouragement and guidance on the path to personal growth.

10. Embracing Personal Growth Opportunities:

Actively seeking opportunities for learning, self-improvement, and new experiences fosters a growth-oriented mindset that aligns with abundance.

11. Taking Inspired Action:

Embracing abundance also requires taking inspired action towards personal and professional goals. Action aligned with positive beliefs and intentions is a key component of manifesting abundance.

12. Embracing Abundance in All Areas of Life:

Abundance isn't limited to financial wealth; it encompasses love, joy, health, creativity, and overall well-being. Embracing abundance in all aspects of life leads to a more holistic and fulfilling existence.

13. Committing to Continuous Growth:

Overcoming limiting beliefs and embracing abundance is an ongoing journey. This commitment to continuous personal growth and self-improvement is essential for maintaining an abundant mindset amidst life's inevitable challenges.

In essence, overcoming limiting beliefs and embracing abundance is a profound inner journey that involves introspection, courage, and a commitment to personal empowerment. By replacing scarcity-based beliefs with those rooted in abundance, individuals can unlock their full potential and create a life rich in fulfillment, joy, and prosperity.

The role of gratitude and giving back in wealth accumulation

The role of gratitude and giving back in wealth accumulation is a multifaceted and deeply transformative aspect of personal and financial growth. This topic delves into the profound connection between gratitude, generosity, and the accumulation of wealth, examining how embracing these principles can enrich both material abundance and personal fulfillment. Here's a comprehensive exploration of this transformational relationship:

1. Gratitude as a Foundation for Wealth Accumulation:

Gratitude serves as a fundamental cornerstone in the process of wealth accumulation. By cultivating a mindset of appreciation for present circumstances, individuals are able to recognize and harness the abundance already present in their lives. This positive perspective creates an energetic foundation conducive to attracting further wealth.

2. Shifting from Scarcity to Abundance:

Gratitude facilitates the shift from a scarcity mindset—focused on perceived lack and limitations—to one rooted in abundance. This shift in perspective opens the individual to greater opportunities, creativity, and resourcefulness, thereby fostering a wealth-conscious mindset.

3. Cultivating Abundance Through Generosity:

Paradoxically, the act of giving back and sharing one's resources with others contributes to the expansion of wealth. Generosity aligns individuals with the flow of abundance, recognizing that there is always enough to share and that giving fosters a cycle of receiving in return.

4. Building Social and Emotional Wealth:

Beyond monetary riches, acts of giving and expressions of gratitude contribute to the accrual of social and emotional wealth. Building meaningful relationships and experiencing the joy of positively impacting others' lives adds richness and depth to one's overall wealth portfolio.

5. Enhancing Well-Being and Fulfillment:

Engaging in acts of gratitude and giving back has been linked to enhanced psychological well-being and life satisfaction. The sense of purpose and fulfillment derived from contributing to the welfare of others is invaluable in the pursuit of holistic wealth.

6. Attracting Greater Opportunities:

Individuals who embody gratitude and prioritize giving often find themselves magnetizing new opportunities, connections, and ventures, leading to enhanced financial and professional success. The practice of giving back can open doors to new partnerships and ventures that contribute to wealth accumulation.

7. Networking and Collaboration:

Acts of gratitude and giving create a positive and abundant reputation, fostering strong networks and collaborative partnerships. These connections are instrumental in creating opportunities for wealth accumulation through joint ventures, referrals, and shared knowledge.

8. Reinforcing Positive Money Mindsets:

Integrating gratitude and giving into one's financial journey reinforces positive money mindsets and attitudes towards wealth. This contributes to sound financial decision-making and the ability to appreciate and preserve wealth once accumulated.

9. Contributing to a Culture of Prosperity:

When individuals and communities practice gratitude and giving back, they contribute to a collective culture of prosperity. This fosters an environment where abundance is celebrated, shared, and perpetuated, benefiting all members of society.

In essence, gratitude and the act of giving back play integral roles in wealth accumulation, transcending mere financial gain to encompass holistic prosperity. By embracing these principles, individuals can transform their relationship with wealth, cultivate a mindset of abundance, and experience the profound fulfillment

that comes from enriching the lives of
both themselves and others.

CONCLUSION

"Sustaining Financial Freedom - A Journey Towards Abundance and Wealth" encapsulates a comprehensive strategy for individuals seeking to cultivate and maintain lasting financial independence. Through this guide, readers are presented with a wealth of foundational principles and actionable steps to lay the groundwork for sustainable wealth accumulation. The book underscores the significance of deliberate planning, strategic decision-making, and a mindset of abundance in fostering enduring financial security.

One of the central tenets elucidated in the book is the pivotal role of creating and adhering to prudent budgeting practices and wise financial management. By cultivating a disciplined approach to spending and saving, individuals can effectively harness their financial resources and gradually pave the way towards prosperity. Furthermore, the text illuminates the importance of strategic investment as a means to grow wealth over time, emphasizing the need for informed decision-making and a long-term perspective in building a robust financial portfolio.

Moreover, "Sustaining Financial Freedom" highlights the imperative of embracing a mindset of abundance as opposed to scarcity. This shift in perspective fosters a proactive and optimistic outlook towards wealth accumulation, empowering individuals to seek out opportunities and capitalize on their strengths. By nurturing an abundant mindset, readers can break free from limiting beliefs and take confident strides towards financial freedom.

Diversification and risk management are also underscored as critical components of any sustainable wealth-building plan. Through prudent diversification of assets and the careful management of risks, individuals can safeguard their financial well-being against unforeseen market fluctuations and economic downturns. Additionally, the book stresses the significance of long-term planning, advocating for the crafting of a comprehensive wealth-building roadmap that spans across different life stages and contingencies.

Central to the book's message is the notion that financial freedom is not merely a destination but rather a lifestyle anchored in intentional and disciplined actions. By creating a personalized wealth-building plan aligned with their unique circumstances and aspirations, individuals can set themselves on a trajectory towards sustained prosperity. This plan encompasses short-term and long-term financial goals, providing a roadmap to navigate through various milestones and challenges on the path to financial freedom.

Furthermore, "Sustaining Financial Freedom" champions the value of ongoing education, adaptability, and continuous improvement in relation to financial matters. The book underscores the importance of staying informed about evolving economic trends and investment opportunities, promoting a dynamic approach to wealth-building that embraces change and innovation. By committing to a lifelong journey of learning and growth, individuals can equip themselves with the insights and skills needed to navigate the complexities of the financial landscape.

In conclusion, "Sustaining Financial Freedom" stands as a guiding beacon for individuals desiring to foster enduring wealth and financial security. Its emphasis on foundational wealth-building principles, personalized planning, and the perpetual pursuit of financial freedom highlights the significance of deliberate, proactive action in achieving lasting abundance. By internalizing these principles and dedicating themselves to a lifelong journey of growth and refinement, readers can forge a path towards sustained financial freedom and embrace a future characterized by prosperity and abundance.

www.ingramcontent.com/pod-product-compliance
Lightning Source LLC
Chambersburg PA
CBHW060050260726
48658CB00004B/1249